PSALM 91
For Children
GOD'S UMBRELLA OF PROTECTION

Peggy Joyce Ruth

Printed in the United States of America
Impact Christian Books, Inc.
332 Leffingwell Ave.,
Kirkwood, MO 63122
314 822 3309
www.impactchristianbooks.com

My sincere appreciation to:
Marcus Stallworth of Dallas, Texas, for the cover design
Gregory Stallworth of Dallas, Texas, for the illustrations
Carolyn Brandenburg and Lynda Low for editing
Living Word Christian Academy Students for specialized editing
My brother, Dr. James Crow, for picture editing
My daughter, Angelia, for manuscript design
Family and Friends for their support and help

ISBN # 0-89228-157-X

Contents

To the Parents

Do you remember the summertime when you were growing up—lying in the backyard as you discovered everything imaginable in those beautiful, huge, white puffy clouds passing overhead? We had cares, of course, the biggest of which was talking mom into letting us have the cute little mutt that had surprised Mrs. Jones that morning on her doorstep as she went out to retrieve the morning paper. For most of us, cancer was something that we knew was terrible, but only because we had heard about some remote acquaintance having it. And, of course, we knew there were natural disasters—but they were some place in India, or maybe in faraway China.

I didn't even know there was a war going on until my dad was suddenly leaving to be gone a long time, and mother sat me down to explain, in a very vague sort of way, his reason for having to be away from us. It never crossed my mind to question his coming back.

TODAY IS A DIFFERENT STORY. Preschoolers know more about what is happening in the news than I knew when I was in Junior High School. First graders are plagued because of the worried look on their mom's face as she (the single parent) struggles to put in a few extra hours that week to make ends meet, until the next paycheck is due. The TV is the baby sitter, so they are privy to every ugly, disgusting thing imaginable. Drugs, AIDES, cancer, heart disease... are everyday occurrences in their little world. Few have escaped having some relative's house, if not their own, destroyed by some natural disaster. Tornado, flood, hurricane, earthquake... are all very common terms, indeed. And we wonder why children today are so prone to fears and worry.

A prime example is a child I'm familiar with who pulls her little eyelashes out when she becomes anxious, and a little boy who wrings his hands when he gets fearful over tormenting fear pictures of his mother and dad getting killed in a car accident. We get calls constantly from parents who cannot understand why their child has nightmares and can't go to sleep. Have you noticed that there is not nearly as much laughter among children as there once was? Is there an answer?

Yes, there is! It is the same answer that God gave me to give to adults whose *hearts are failing* them *because of fears,* and whose minds are being comforted only by the temporary relief of some prescription drug—or worse yet, some street drug. God anointed me to write a book called *Psalm 91 God's Umbrella of Protection* to inform Christians of their covenant right to God's protection. Hundreds of adults have written to me, saying that their lives have been transformed by the message in that book, but I am becoming keenly aware that children need that message equally as much as adults. I think you will find this new book, *Psalm 91 for Young People,* to be one of the most beneficial things you have ever gotten for your child.

They hear the problems everyday. Now they can hear the answer God has given that can equip them for a fearless, abundantly victorious life.

8

Young People—Let's Have a Little Talk Before You Start Reading Your Book!

Do you know what fear is? Fear is a thought that the old devil puts in your mind to make you feel sad and scared. Did you know that God does not want you to be afraid of anything? Three hundred and sixty six times in the Bible God tells us, *"Be not afraid!"* Have you ever told someone something that many times? If you did, you must have really wanted them to hear what you had to say. Don't you think maybe God wanted you to know how to get rid of all those old fear thoughts from the devil if He went to the trouble to tell you 366 times not to be afraid? Of course, He does!

Many years ago I started praying and asking God if there was some way for a Christian to be protected from the bad things that were happening in the world. I didn't want to have cancer or a heart attack. I hoped there was a way to keep from having a bad car wreck or from having my house blown away in a tornado. When I thought of all those things, I would get frightened, and I would pray really hard for God to answer my prayer.

Then one day God showed me in a dream to go to Psalm 91. He told me that was where I would find the answer I had been looking for. I nearly tore the pages in my Bible—I was turning them so fast to get to Psalm 91, so I could see what it said. And when I read it, my eyes almost bugged out of my head because, there it was—the answer I had been praying for. I had never read it before, but it had been there all the time—a promise for protection for all of God's children so that we would not have to fear all the evil things that are happening in the world. When I read that Psalm I was so happy that I cried. Do you remember how you felt when you got something that you had been wanting with all of your heart? Maybe for you guys, it was a bicycle! For you girls, it might have been a dress that you had been really desiring. But do you remember how it felt? You were just happy all over—so happy that you couldn't quit smiling. That is how I felt when I first turned to Psalm 91 and read it out loud. I was so happy that God had answered my prayer and shown me a way to come out of my fears. So I started studying Psalm 91 every day, and the more I believed it, the better it worked.

Then God told me that it was not just a promise for me. He told me to write a book so all of His children could hear about His promise of protection and quit being afraid. **This is going to be one of the most important things you will ever learn**, so turn in your Bible to Psalm 91. Get ready to be blessed with a promise from God that will protect you for the rest of your life, as I share what God showed me that day in my dream.

Chapter 1

Where is Your Secret Hiding Place?

*Those who go to God Most High for safety will
be protected by God All-Powerful.* Psalm 91: 1

Think for just a minute where more than
anyplace else in the world you like to be when you
want to feel protected and peaceful. I remember
when I was a little girl and would wake up in the
middle of the night and feel afraid, I would tip-toe
down to my mother and dad's room and very
quietly slip in bed with them. As I lay there
silently listening to them breathe and feeling all
cozy and protected—before I knew it, the fear was
gone, and I would be sound asleep.

I am sure that you can think of something that
makes you feel secure. When I think of feeling
secure and protected, I have another childhood
memory that always comes to my mind. My
parents would often take me and my younger
brother and sister to a lake. There was a wonderful
place to fish for perch that very few people knew
about, and we children loved to perch fish. It was
such a thrill to see the cork begin to bobble and
then suddenly go completely out of sight. There
were very few things that I liked better than

jerking back on that old cane pole and landing a huge perch. Dad had a good reason for having us catch those perch. They were what he used for bait on the trotline that he had stretched out across one of the secret coves at the lake.

Dad would drive the boat over to the place where his trotline was located. Then he would cut off the boat motor and inch the boat across the water as he "ran the trotline." That is what he called it when he would hold onto the trotline with his hands and pull the boat alongside all the hooks that he had baited, in hopes that he had caught a big catfish. A trotline was like having about 25 fishing poles baited and placed all the way across the lake.

I loved to perch fish, but it was an even greater thrill when Dad would get to a place where the trotline rope would begin to jerk almost out of his hand. That meant that he had hooked a fish. It was then that all three of us children would watch—wide eyed—as Dad would wrestle with that line until finally, in victory, he would flip that huge catfish over the side of the boat right at our feet. Money could never buy that kind of excitement! The circus and carnival, all rolled up into one, couldn't give us that kind of a thrill.

One of those outings proved to be more exciting than most—turning out to be an action-packed experience that I will never forget. It had been a beautiful day when we started out, but by the time we had finished our perch fishing and were headed toward the place on the lake where Dad had the trotline, everything changed. A storm came up on the lake so quickly that there was no time to get back to the boat dock. The sky turned black, lightning was flashing and drops of rain were falling so hard that they stung our skin when they hit. Then moments later we were in the middle of a hailstorm with large marble-sized hail.

I could see the fear in my mother's eyes, and I knew we were in danger. But before I had time to wonder what we were going to do, Dad had driven the boat to the rugged shoreline of the only island on the lake. There are many boat docks that surround the island now, but back then it looked like an abandoned island with absolutely no place to hide from the storm.

In just moments Dad had us all out of the boat and ordered the three of us to lie down beside our mother on the ground. Quickly pulling a canvas tarp out of the bottom of the boat, he knelt down on the ground beside us and pulled that tarp up over all five of us. That storm raged outside the homemade tent he had put over us—the rain beat down, the lightning flashed, and the thunder rolled—but all I could think about was how it felt to have his arms around us. There was a certain peace that is hard to explain as we lay there under the protection of the shield my father had provided. In fact, I had never felt as safe and secure in my entire life. I can remember thinking that I wished that the storm would last forever. I didn't want anything to spoil the wonderful security that I felt that day—there in our *secret hiding place.* Feeling my father's strong, protective arms around me, I wanted it never to end.

Maybe you have a secret hideout where you feel all safe and secure when you get in it, hidden away from the whole world—or maybe you feel secure when you are alone in your own room. Those places where you feel protected are nice, but they cannot always keep you safe from everything. However, there is a place of shelter that will keep you protected from every evil this world has ever known. **God says that He is a place of real safety from any bad thing you can think of in the whole earth—if you will run to Him**. How do you run to God? You don't run there with your feet. **You run to God with your heart!** You are running to God every time that you think about Him—every time you tell Him that you love Him. If you believe that God is telling you the truth when He says that He is a place of safety where you can be protected, then He is pleased. Jesus wants you to be protected with all of His heart.

Chapter 2

I Must Learn What To Say...

I will say to the Lord, "You are my place of
safety and protection. You are my God, and
I trust You."   Psalm 91: 2

Did you notice that God says that you are
supposed to *say out loud* that *God* is your *place of*
safety and protection? He wants you to tell Him
that you trust Him. It is not enough to just think
about God. When you say God's Word out loud
and believe it—something happens out there in the
unseen world where the angels live.

It is easy to see why God likes for us to say it
out loud to Him. How would you feel if you lived
in the house with your mother and father, and you
saw them everyday, but they never said anything
out loud to you? That wouldn't feel very good,
would it? When you tell God that you believe Him
when He says He will protect you—God hears it,
His angels hear it and the devil also hears it. Then
God can say, *"Devil, you cannot hurt him. He*
believes My Word, and he is protected," and God's
angels go to work to protect you as well.

So many times we are doing everything we can think of to protect ourselves, and, to a point, that is not bad. It is good to eat healthy food and obey safety rules and even go to a doctor when your parents think it is the right thing to do. God is pleased when you do things that are wise, but those things cannot always protect you. God is the only One who can protect you from *whatever* the problem might be.

Do you know why God calls us His sheep? It's because a sheep is the only animal that doesn't have any protection on its own. It is not like a dog that can bark away his enemies or a skunk that can spray out a bad odor to keep from being bothered. Some animals have sharp teeth to protect themselves, but a sheep doesn't have anything to protect himself—**except the shepherd**. We are God's sheep, and Jesus is our good Shepherd. He wants us to know that He is our protector. Just like the shepherds on the hillside protect their sheep, Jesus wants to protect us.

When I get afraid that something bad is going to happen, I say out loud, "*Jesus, You are my Shepherd, and I am Your sheep. I know you will protect me because You promised that in Psalm 91, so I am not going to fear. In Jesus' Name I tell that fear to leave me alone.*"

When my niece, Julie, was ten years old she got thrown from a horse, cracking her skull like an egg shell, and the doctors told us not to expect her to live through the night. It is really hard to stand on God's Word when you are getting bad reports from educated doctors, because it is easy to think that they are always right. And Julie was a terrible sight. When the nurses pushed her past us on a stretcher, I didn't even know it was Julie. Her face was just one big bubble of blood, but her mother and dad had made the decision to believe God more than they believed anything else. They knew that God's Word says that *Jesus died on the cross and redeemed us from the curse (sickness, disease, poverty, accidents...)*—**so they kept saying,** "*Julie will live and not die to declare the wonderful works of God.*" The doctors thought we were crazy—they were so sure she couldn't live in that condition. And even if she did live, they said she would be brain damaged and would never be able to see or hear well again. But the family refused to give up on the promises of God.

To the surprise of all the doctors and nurses, Julie did live through the night, and not only lived, but in a few days she was miraculously dismissed from the hospital with no brain damage, perfect eyesight and perfect hearing. The doctors were shocked, and the nurses called her *their little miracle girl.* Don't forget that Psalm 91 is **your** covenant of protection, as well.

God's Word is true, and He is faithful to do what He promises if we will put our complete trust in Him and continue to say only what His word says.

***

Before our little grandson was born the doctor said that he had died. And while our daughter in law, Sloan, was having surgery, the surgeon even looked around to prove the baby wasn't there. But Sloan would not believe that. She was trusting God to protect her little baby and keep him alive. She would put her hand on her stomach and obey verse two by saying out loud, "*My baby will live and not die and tell all about the wonderful things that God does.*" Later when she went back for a checkup after her surgery, the doctor said, "*I don't understand how it happened, but you still have a baby, and he's alive. He is not dead.*"

Our grandson is eight years old now, and his name is Cullen. I am so glad his mother believed God's Word and confessed it out loud, because I love my grandson. I don't know what I would do without him.

God wants you to believe His Word more than you believe some person who is telling you something different—no matter how smart and important you think that individual is. God is faithful to His Word if we trust Him.

Chapter 3

No More Traps of Satan

God will save you from hidden traps and from
deadly diseases.   Psalm 91: 3

Have you ever gone to a movie and seen a trapper hide a big steel trap under the leaves to try to capture an animal? When the animal steps into that trap, it snaps shut, and he's caught.

Did you know that the devil has traps set for each one of us? They are not steel traps like animal trappers use—Satan sometimes uses *spiritual* traps. Do you know what a spiritual trap is? There are many different kinds. When Satan tempts you to sin—that *temptation* is one kind of trap. If you fall for the temptation and sin, it is like getting caught in the trap, and bad things happen.

Let's think of some examples: have you ever wanted something, and when no one was looking you were tempted to take it? That is a trap of the devil. Maybe you've broken something before and pretended someone else did it so you wouldn't get into trouble. *Not telling the truth* is a trap of the enemy. When you get tempted to get angry and fight with a friend—or say something unkind—that's also a trap that the devil has put in front of you. But God promises that He will save you from hidden traps. How does He do that? Every time you are tempted to do anything wrong, God wants you to think about what Jesus would do, and how you could do it right instead of falling for that temptation. **It takes courage to do it right, but God will give you the strength to say 'no' every time you are tempted.** That is one of the ways God saves you from those hidden traps. He gives you the strength to say 'no,' but He won't make you. You have to choose to do that yourself.

Try writing this scripture out on a small card — *I can do all things through Christ because He gives me strength (Phil 4:13).* Carry it in your pocket, and pull it out and read it often. The Word of God is a real weapon. It is a *spiritual* weapon, and when you say it out loud and mean it, temptations leave.

> *We do live in the world. But we do not fight the same way that the world fights. We fight with weapons that are different from those the world uses. Our weapons have power from God. These weapons can destroy the enemy's strong places. We destroy men's arguments. And we destroy every proud thing that raises itself against the knowledge of God. We capture every thought and make it give up and obey Christ.* 2 Corinthians 10: 3-5

Sometimes the traps of the enemy are *physical* traps sent to destroy you. In the town where we live there is a sulfur spring, and when we were young there was a swimming pool filled with sulfur water. My dad had a back injury, and the doctor wanted him to float in that warm sulfur water every day. We loved the idea because Dad bought season swimming passes for all of us, and the moment he got home from work we would all head for the pool to swim while Dad floated.

My brother, Jim, was about five at the time, and, in spite of the fact that he had become a very good swimmer because of those daily outings, Mother still made him wear a life jacket. Back then it was one of those big, bulky, orange jackets that we called *water wings*. Under normal circumstances that life jacket would probably have been a good idea because Jim was swimming all over the place, and it was a huge pool with murky sulfur water. Today we are used to pools that are kept crystal clear with all the chlorine.

There was a large concrete platform out in the middle of the pool with a diving board, and it was fun to see who could hold his breath and swim under the platform from one side to the other. However, on one of our daily swims Jim decided to swim underwater the full **length** of the platform. He intended to start from the deep end of the diving board, swim underwater to the steps on the other end, go under the bottom rung and come up on the other side. That meant when he got to the steps he had to pull himself down to that last rung—life jacket and all—by holding onto the underwater ladder and forcing himself down by sheer strength. Without a life jacket that little adventure would probably have been OK, but when he tried to force himself under that last step, the life jacket caught and trapped him three feet under the water. Our little sister, Sandra, who was two years younger than Jim, kept saying, *"Where is Bubba?"* When someone finally got around to paying attention to what she was saying, the panic was on. We began looking everywhere for him in that giant pool. It was my father who finally caught a faint glimpse of the orange life jacket through that murky sulfur water and dove down, working frantically until he was able to get the jacket dislodged. He had to literally push Jim further down in the water to free the jacket from the steps before he could bring him up.

No one knew for sure how long Jim was under the water, but it had to have been several minutes. He had already held his breath for the time it took to swim lengthwise under the platform—the time it took to force himself under the steps—the time it took for him to be missed—and then the time it took for my father to get him out of the trap. When Jim was asked if he was scared, he answered, *"No, I knew my daddy would come and get me out of the trap, but I didn't like it when he pushed me further under the water—I wanted up."*

Have you ever been trapped somewhere? That is a really frightening feeling, and it's easy to panic during those times. I am so thankful that Jim didn't panic. He would probably have drowned.

Guys, the reason I am telling you this story is because it is a perfect example of how we should look to our heavenly Father every time we feel trapped. If we pray and put our trust in God, He will rescue us from the traps that Satan has laid for us. And we also have to trust God and not get into fear when there are things we don't understand. Remember, it was hard for a five year old to understand why his dad was pushing him further down in the water, but that was the only way to get him out of the trap. Our heavenly father will never do anything except what is best for us.

***

Verse three of Psalm 91 also says that He will save you from deadly diseases (pestilence). Can you think of some deadly diseases that destroy people? Of course you can—cancer, heart disease, diabetes, leukemia... The world may laugh at you for believing God, but He promises to protect you from those things. This verse promises protection from two directions: from the *temptation* traps to get you to sin—and from things sent *to hurt you physically*. But it is up to you to believe God's promise to help you overcome from either direction.

Chapter 4

Under His Wings!
🕊 🕊 🕊

*God will protect you like a bird spreading its
wings over its young.*　　　Psalm 91: 4a

If you could see in the unseen spiritual world
where the angels live, you would be able to see a
covering that God has over you—if you believe
this promise. I like it when God paints a picture so
I can understand His Word better. Have you ever
seen a mother bird spread her wings over the baby
birds in the nest to protect them? That is a picture
of what God does for you when you run to Him for
protection.

My husband and I live in the country, and one
spring our old mother hen hatched some baby
chicks. One afternoon when the little chicks were
scattered all over the yard, I suddenly saw the
shadow of a hawk overhead. Then I noticed
something very interesting that taught me a lesson
I will never forget. That mother hen did not run to
those little chicks and jump on top of them to try to
cover them with her wings. No! Instead she
squatted down, spread out her wings and began to
cluck. And those little chicks came running *to her*

from every direction to get under those outstretched wings. Then she pulled her wings down tight, tucking every little chick safely under her. To get to those babies the hawk would have to go through the mother hen.

When I think of those baby chicks running to their mother, it reminds me that we have to run to God. He does not run all over the place trying to put His covering over us. He said, *"I have made protection available. You run to Me!"* And when we do run to God in faith, the enemy will have to go through God to get to us, and that would be impossible. When you think about that, it should make you feel very safe and protected.

Chapter 5

Behind His Shield!
♥ ♥ ♥

God's faithfulness is a shield...(NAS) Psalm 91: 4b

I want you to picture a big shield out in front of
you—one so big that you can hide behind it, and
no one can even see you. That shield is God
Himself. **Your faith in those promises and in
God's faithfulness to do what He says becomes
a shield** in front of you to protect you from
dangerous things with which the enemy tries to
hurt you.

Some people think they can't be protected
because they know they are not good enough.
None of us is good enough, but Jesus is good
enough for all of us. Isn't it wonderful to know
that it is God's loving mercy that makes all this
protection possible? I'm so glad He doesn't give
us what we deserve. We should never quit
thanking God for giving us all this protection, even
though we don't deserve it—and it is only possible
because Jesus took our sin and our punishment on
Himself on the cross. He took the punishment that
we deserved.

I knew this young man who was careless and caught some grease on fire, and it could very easily have burned down the house if his older brother had not come in the nick of time and put the fire out.   As the older brother was cleaning up the mess, the father came in, and, thinking that the older brother was the one who had been careless, gave him the punishment.   The younger brother watched as his brother, without saying a word, took the punishment that he knew he deserved. That is a beautiful picture of love, and that is exactly what our older brother, Jesus, did for each one of us. All we have to do is be truly sorry for our sin and put all our trust in Him.

It is God who has made you part of Christ Jesus. Christ has become wisdom for us from God. Christ is the reason we are right with God and have freedom from sin; Christ is the reason we are holy.
I Corinthians 1: 30

You can never be good enough on your own. Your righteousness and the good things you try to do will never be enough. Jesus died for you and took your sin and punishment because He loved you so much.   There is a difference, however, between making a mistake every once in awhile and asking God to forgive you, and doing wrong things because you want to.   When you sin on purpose it is called willful sin.   Self will and selfishness and rebellion will keep you out from behind the shield. And when you are not behind the shield, the enemy can see you and hurt you. You will also find yourself out from behind the shield when you *forget* about God's promises.

When our associate pastor's daughters, Christy and Ginger, were young, they lived in Green River, Wyoming. On July 4th they begged their dad to let them sleep outside in the tent. It's cold in Wyoming at night, so they were zipped up in sleeping bags inside a tightly closed tent, when fireworks started exploding all around them.

Have you ever had a fear picture in your mind of something bad happening? The fireworks were so loud and hitting so close to the tent that Christy and Ginger began to have a fear picture of the tent going up in flames and catching even their bedrolls on fire. That is a terrible feeling. They were so frightened that they couldn't even get up enough courage to run into the house for protection. But their mom and dad had taught them about Psalm 91. So they began to speak those verses out loud, *"We will not be afraid because God's faithfulness is a shield of protection around us."* Even before the fireworks ceased, peace flooded the tent, and they fell asleep. The next morning when they went outside, they realized that God had truly protected them. There were 27 large bottle rockets all around their tent. God heard their cry and put His shield of protection around them.

Chapter 6

I Will Not Fear What Another Person Can Do to Me!
🚑 🚑 🚑

You will not fear any danger by night. Psalm 91: 5a

Verses five and six cover **every bad thing in the world,** and all those bad things are divided into four groups.   Let's look at each of these four groups one at the time. The first group in verse five is called ***danger by night.*** The Hebrew word is ***terror*** *by night.* This group includes all the evil that comes through bad people: kidnappers, robbers, murderers... Think of some other things that bad people do—because this first group of evil that God calls *terror by night* includes every really bad thing that *another person* can do to harm you. But God says, *"Don't be afraid of any of those bad things that people can do to you— because I will protect you.*

Do you remember how many times the Bible tells you not to be afraid? 366 times! God must have wanted you to hear Him when He said, *"Don't be afraid!"* Did you know that God has given you the *Name of Jesus* and the *Holy Scriptures* to use as a weapon to fight the devil and bad spirits that work through evil people? But those weapons will do you no good if you don't know how to use them. Most of you know how to use a physical weapon. If I handed you a gun or a knife you would not try to use your foot and your big toe to make it work. Of course not! That sounds silly! You know to use your hand and fingers to operate physical weapons. But most people do not know what part of the body to use to make spiritual weapons work. Do you know? *You operate spiritual weapons with your mouth and your tongue*. Every word you speak is a spiritual weapon--either for good or for evil.

Did you know that your words are very powerful? Every word you speak with faith will change things for good or for bad. That is why it is so important to say what God's Word says. If you say negative things that go against God's Word, you bring negative, evil things into your life. For example—when you say things like, *"I'm always sick,"* or *"I hate my brother (or sister),"* or *"I don't want to read God's Word"* or *"God let me down"*—you are using Satan's weapons. What comes out of your mouth is firing either God's weapon or Satan's weapon. Did you know that?

Life and death are in the power of the tongue.
Proverbs 18: 21

When things are going wrong you have to choose
to believe God's Word more than you believe what
you see—even more than you believe what the
whole world is saying, if they are not going God's
Way. And you have *to keep saying* what God's
Word says. Sometimes that is hard to do when bad
things look real, but God's Word is more powerful
than anything in this world. It can overcome any
problem that comes. Gravity is a good example.
Everyone knows that gravity is real, but there is a
higher law called aerodynamics that can override the
law of gravity and let a plane fly through the air.
Gravity is still there, but the higher law of
aerodynamics is stronger. In the same way Satan's
attacks are as real as gravity, but his attacks can also
be overcome by a higher law called *Faith in God's
Word* because God's Word is stronger.

We have a friend named Julee, and a man broke
into her apartment and tried to harm her. He was a
big, strong man, but she started saying, *"You cannot
hurt me. God promises in Psalm 91 to protect me if I
trust Him. So I tell you to leave me alone in Jesus
Name."* She had to say it many times, but the man
finally got scared, and he left her apartment without
harming her at all. *What another person can do
to hurt you* is called *terror*, but God says that you do
not have to be afraid of the terror. Thank God for
His higher law. When you believe the Word and
decide that you are going to say it out of your
mouth—no matter how long it takes—you will
finally win.

Chapter 7

Satan's Arrows Won't Hurt Me
←↑↓→

*You will not be afraid of the **arrow** during the day!*
Psalm 91: 5b

The second group of evil—listed in verse five—is the **arrow**. An arrow is something that pierces or wounds you. It can be sent to hurt your body *physically*, or to hurt your feelings *emotionally* or to pull you away from God *spiritually*. The enemy sends these arrows on purpose and tries to aim them at the spot that will hurt the most. Some arrows are like a temptation to get you to sin—perhaps in an area where you're still losing your temper—or an area where maybe you're selfish—or where you get your feelings hurt too easily—or an area where you still rebel against your parents—or where you are still into fear. Think about some areas where you are not very strong in God's Word. Those will often be the main target. Let's look at some examples:

It is easy for some people to start eating without thinking about praying over their food, if they don't know the reason why God tells them to bless their food and water. God's Word says that it takes sickness away from the food and purifies it when you pray over it and bless it. There are a lot of bad things like chemicals and preservatives in our food and water today—that's why it is important to pray to God for protection.

***

Do you sometimes feel *like a failure* and get discouraged when you make bad grades in school? Did you know that there are scripture promises that you can confess to do well in school? Satan sometimes sends arrows like *distracting thoughts* when you are taking a test or trying to study. Start saying what God's Word says—"*No weapon used against me will defeat me." (Isaiah 54: 17), "In all these things I have the full victory through Christ who loves me." (Romans 8: 37)* The Word of God is a spiritual weapon and it can destroy those arrows sent from the enemy to hurt you.

***

Another kind of arrow is a *difficulty* or a *problem* that the enemy tries to give you. Often people don't realize that many of the problems that come are actually *arrows* sent from the devil. Sometimes those arrows come through other people and sometimes through circumstances.

Many years ago my husband was in business with his father. They owned a company that bottled Pepsi. One of the other bottling companies in town got a new manager, and he told everyone that he was going to spend as much money as necessary to put us out of business. It is good to have competition if everyone plays fair, but this new manager started doing some unfair things to get storeowners to send our vending machines back to us, so that they would use his. He even had our Pepsi lines cut. We wouldn't have known he was the one doing that if our neighbor, who worked for the other company, hadn't told us what was going on. We were losing a lot of money. In fact, it was so bad that for a while it looked as if we might go broke. But God reminded us of this verse five and told us *not to be afraid of the arrow* (the evil things that were being done to us).

Finally that other manager quit his job and left town, and gradually our business started doing better. We found out later that all the money he was spending to try to hurt our business made him run out of money first. God had protected us from the arrows (the problems) that the devil was sending through that manager.

***

Another arrow that so many young people have to deal with is *harassment*. Nearly every school has a bully, and it can take all the fun out of going if you are always being bothered by someone bullying you. It is one of Satan's favorite tricks to use another person to irritate you and rob your joy.

Sometimes that person is having trouble at home or he's unhappy about something, and the enemy tricks him into taking his problems out on other people. Instead of being angry, do what the Bible says and begin praying for him. Prayer is a powerful spiritual weapon, and it can change impossible situations.

***

One of the devil's favorite arrows is to hurt a child by causing him to lose a pet. A young man in our Children's Church had his dog disappear. That hurt because he was very fond of that dog, but instead of getting all down in the dumps, he started praying and believing God to help him find his dog. Everyone else in the family had given up, but he was determined, and he kept thanking God for its safe return. Suddenly one day, there was his little dog on the door step—waiting for food. Another boy lost his dog, and God gave him an even better one. It is the devil's trick to make you get angry with God when something doesn't go right, but it is never God who allows bad things. If you keep trusting God, you won't be disappointed.

***

Sometimes the arrow is aimed at your money, and the *problem* is *not having enough* for something you need or want. When we were building our home in the country, Bill wanted to make a huge chicken pen out of wire mesh so that he could raise some ducks and chickens and pheasants.

We were having to use our faith to believe for the money to build the house, so Jack told Bill that this was a good time for him to learn how to believe God himself for what he needed. Several days later he got off the school bus, so excited he could hardly talk. On the way home that day he had seen huge rolls of chicken wire in the city park. It had been taken down from around the tennis courts and replaced with chain link fencing. Bill called the City Hall, and they told him he could have every bit of the chicken wire if he would haul it off. There was enough wire to build a huge pen and to also put wire over the top so the birds couldn't fly out. So often kids put pressure on their parents for money, but this shows that you can pray to God on your own. Bill prayed and used his own faith rather than putting pressure on his dad. He knew he had a heavenly Father! God will give you creative ideas to meet your needs when Satan is trying to hold back your money.

The Lord would not have made this promise to protect you from the arrows of the enemy if He had not intended you to believe Him and to get the victory.

Chapter 8

Disease Won't Hurt Me
Ϋ Ϋ Ϋ

*You will not be afraid of diseases...*Psalm 91: 6a

The third group of evil that God named was
diseases. The Hebrew word is **pestilence**. This is
the only evil that God named twice. He told you in
verse three that He would save you from deadly
diseases, and now He is telling you again in verse
six that you are not to be afraid of deadly diseases,
because they will not come near you.

Does your mother or your father ever tell you
something more than once? Why? Because they
really want you to hear what they're saying! God
wants you to pay attention to what He is saying to
you here. Since there are so many horrible
diseases in the world, it is easy to think that it's
normal to be sick. Some people think that
everyone has to be sick once in awhile, but that is
not true. It is not natural to be sick, but Satan
wants you to think it is, so he can put a sickness on
you. Sometimes it is hard, though, to believe these
promises in Psalm 91, because we're around
people in the world who do not believe God's
Word.

But we need to change our thinking until our thoughts line up with the Bible. Matthew 8: 16 says that many people were brought to Jesus, and He healed all who were sick. Then verse 17 says that He did these things to make come true what Isaiah the prophet said: "*Jesus took our diseases on Himself. And He bore our pain for us.*" If He bore it for us, we don't have to bear it again.

Even if the world doesn't believe in the healing power of Jesus, that does not keep it from being true. And the person who has faith in God's promise to heal will be able to enjoy healing every time. Some people think that faith is hard, but that is because they think faith is a *feeling*. **Faith is not a feeling. Faith is simply *choosing* to believe what God says in His Word and refusing to doubt.**

The arrows we talked about in chapter seven are sometimes aimed against people when they are first born—like at the times of the birth of Moses and Jesus, when all the boy babies were killed because Satan was trying to get rid of Moses and God's Son. When our son, Bill, was born, there was a disease that came against him to try to take his life. Bill was born with the same membrane disease in his lungs that had killed President Kennedy's baby just a short time before.

None of the hospital staff expected Bill to live, and he was placed in an incubator for over a month. Think how hard it would be—not to be able to get close to or even touch your newborn baby for over a month. We would go everyday to the hospital and look at him through a huge glass window. We were sad that he was sick, but somehow God gave Jack and me a *gift of faith* to believe that he would live and not die.

It is so much fun to see all the different ways in which God works mysteriously when you are trusting in His Word. Our doctor's two nephews had both died from that same disease, and he had quit practicing medicine for a while to study and try to find a cure for it. In fact, the doctor had only recently started practicing medicine again when Bill was born. So when he discovered that Bill had the exact same disease his nephews had, he started trying everything on Bill that he had read about during his studies. And miraculously, Bill started responding to one of the methods—the Epsom salt enemas. Thanks be to God for this promise in verse six—*you will not be afraid of disease...it will not approach you*—because, instead of losing our baby, we were able to bring home from the hospital a perfectly healed, healthy baby boy.

Many babies, who had famous doctors in large city hospitals, died from that disease, yet our son lived. You can know it was God helping us when we found a small town doctor, who had done all that research until he found a cure for the very disease that Bill had. God works sometimes through human hands, but He is still the One doing the healing.

***

I have a good friend named Joyce. Her stomach got all swollen, and the doctors did tests and told her that she had cancer all in her body. It is very tempting to get into fear when the doctor gives you a bad report, but she chose to believe God's Word more than she believed the report of the doctors. She continued to say out loud that she was healed because *Jesus took her sicknesses and diseases on the cross.* Then another report came back, and the doctors said, *"We don't understand it, but you don't have any cancer in your body."* It pays to believe Jesus because the promises are only for those who believe.

***

When everyone in school is coming down with *upset stomach* and *throw-up or some virus,* don't start thinking that you will probably be the next one to get sick. Do you know what it means to pray a *prevention prayer?* When you prevent something, it means that you keep it from happening. Pray ahead of time and thank God that you can walk in health because Jesus took sickness on the cross. Jesus is the Healer, and it is nice to get healed, but it is even better to stay healthy.

***

One young man got a list of all the healing scriptures and read them onto a cassette tape. Then he would play that tape over and over until it was easy for him to believe God's Word on healing. God has told you that *you don't have to be afraid of diseases.* Let your mind think about that promise over and over until you believe it with all your heart.

53

Chapter 9

I Will Not Fear Destruction

You will not be afraid of the destruction. Psalm 91:6b

The fourth group of evil is called **destruction**. Destruction is the evil over which people have no control—things like storms, floods, fires, car wrecks, etc. The world may call these things *acts of God,* but they are not coming from God.

When Jesus rebuked the storm in Mark 4:39, it became perfectly calm—showing us that God is not the One who sends these natural disasters. Jesus would never have gone against His Father by rebuking something, if God had sent it.

There is no place in the world where you can go and be safe from every destruction—every natural disaster. I am not saying that to put fear on you. I am saying that so you will realize that there is no safe place *in the world* to hide, **but no matter where you are in the world, God says that you can run to His shelter and *not be afraid of the destruction, because it will not come near you.***

One of the favorite testimonies at our church is Skylar Chasteen's miracle story. At four years old he was riding his bike with his older brothers, when he suddenly lost control and went over the side of a cliff. His mother found him tangled in his bike—unconscious, his chin past his shoulder— and he was not breathing. His aunt Cynthia began to pray Psalm 91 over him and to rebuke the enemy of death off of him in Jesus' Name.

On the way to the hospital they would give him rescue breaths. He would breathe for a few minutes, and then quit again. They stopped at the nearest hospital for help, but when the X-rays showed a bad break in the first vertebra in his neck, the doctors sent him by helicopter on to a large hospital in Ft Worth.

His mother continued to thank God that the devil could not destroy Skylar because Psalm 91 said that they *did not have to be afraid of destruction... it would not approach them.*

After much time and more X-rays the doctors in Ft Worth came out with a puzzled look on their faces. They could not find a broken bone in his neck anywhere—even though they had the first set of X-rays to prove that there had been one. They had to admit that it was a miracle. Since the day Skylar left the hospital, he has been a perfectly normal, healthy little boy with no problems and no side effects from the accident. He truly is a miracle because we have a miracle working God.

***

Jack and Bill did not know there was an old underground gas well at the back of our property where they were burning brush. When the fire got over the gas well it literally exploded, sending fire in every direction and setting a nearby field of tall, dry grass into blaze. It didn't take long until the fire was completely out of control. There were no water lines back there at the time, and the barrel of water they had in the back of the pickup didn't even make a dent in the flames.

Jack came flying up to the house to call the fire department, but we lived so far out of town that he knew the fire trucks would never get there in time. (He was concerned that the fire would get to the houses behind the field.) However, when he dashed back, he found Bill covered with ashes and sitting on a tree stump trying to catch his breath— **but the fire was out.** Jack was so shocked that he said, *"How on earth were you able to put out the fire?"* And Bill said, *"I called on God!"*

There was no way that Bill could have put that fire out without God's help. That pasture was bigger than two football fields, with flames spreading in all directions faster than a man can run.

56

It's easy to panic when things get out of
control, but those are the times when it is more
important than ever to call on God. Thank God
for His wonderful promises. And remember that
you, too, can be delivered from destruction. Call
on God. He is always there.

***

Every extreme evil known to man will fall into
one of these four groups in verses five and six:
terror (*evil things that another person can do to
hurt you*), **arrows** (*temptations and evil plans that
Satan sends against you*), **deadly diseases** and
destruction (*natural disasters*). The amazing
thing is that God has told you that He will protect
you from all of these things, if you will trust Him.

There will always be some people who won't
believe these promises, even if you show it to them
in the Bible. But that does not keep the promises
from being true for the ones who do believe. So
don't let anyone talk you out of this covenant. It is
better to trust God than to go by what man says.

Chapter 10

I Will See Thousands Fall!
☒ ☒ ☒

At your side 1,000 people may die, or even 10,000 right beside you. But you will not be hurt.
Psalm 91: 7

There are some people who don't know how to claim these promises. And sometimes it's hard to believe God's Word, when you see people getting sick and dying all around you, but God tells you very plainly here in this verse seven that not everyone is going to believe.

In Luke 4: 27 Jesus said, *"There were many lepers in Israel in the time of Elisha, but none of them was cleansed except Naaman who was a foreigner."* Only Naaman, the Syrian, was healed when he obeyed God in faith. Even God's own people in Israel didn't believe. Not everyone will get the benefits of these promises in Psalm 91— only those who believe God. Jesus said that He could only heal a few sick people in Nazareth, because only those few believed. Many missed getting healed because of their unbelief, but you do not have to be one who misses out if you will believe God.

Have you ever been really frightened when you heard the weather report that a tornado was over your town? Late one night we turned on our radio just as they reported that a tornado was on the ground right behind the country club. That's where we live. The sky was a strange color; everything was still and not a night creature was making a sound. There was so much electricity in the air that our hair felt like it was standing on end.

Jack quickly made us all get our Bibles and start circling the house as we read Psalm 91 and told the storm to *be gone* in Jesus' Name. We did that for a good while until we felt peaceful again. By that time the rain was coming down so hard that it felt like bucketsful instead of drops. But when we walked back into the house the radio announcer was saying, *"This is nothing short of a miracle—the funnel cloud south of the country club has suddenly lifted back in the sky and has vanished before our very eyes."*

People in the world call that a lucky break, but that is not luck. God honors His Word when we believe it and act on it. The next day when our daughter went to school, the teacher asked each student what they were doing while the tornado was overhead. Some had gotten into the bathtub for protection, some were under mattresses and a few of the students were in a storm cellar. When the teacher got to Angelia and asked her what she and her family were doing during the storm, she said, "*My father got us out of bed in our pajamas and had us take our Bibles and walk around the house, quoting Psalm 91 to the storm until it was gone.*" You can imagine how shocked the teacher was when she heard that. Some people just do not know about the protection of the Lord.

***

My friend in Memphis sent me a newspaper article showing the homes that were completely destroyed by a storm that hit their city. She said that when she heard the noise during the night, she jumped out of her bed and started thanking God out loud for His promises from Psalm 91. When daylight came she found that there were many houses destroyed, and huge trees were uprooted all around, but the house where she lived and the trees in her yard had not been harmed by the storm.

God has given you these wonderful promises in Psalm 91 to protect you from every kind of evil that might come, but it is up to you to believe these promises more than you believe what you see with your eyes and hear with your ears. **The good news is that you do not have to be one of the 10,000 who fall, if you will hold fast to God's Word.**

Chapter 11

My Family Can Be Safe!

Nothing bad will happen to you. No disaster will come to your home. Psalm 91: 10

Sometimes it is hard not to worry about your family. Have you ever been tormented with the thought that your mother or your dad might die? That is a horrible feeling, and God does not want you to be in that kind of fear. That is why in verse ten He tells you that *no disaster will come to your family.*

My friend Crystal's son, Jeffery Phillips, was one of the first ones sent to Iraq. Everyday she had been saying the entire Psalm 91 out loud and thanking God for his protection. One day a letter came from the United States government saying that they were very sorry to tell them that their son had been killed in action. When she opened the letter, she was stunned. For a little while she couldn't think what to do. She wanted to call her husband and call all of her friends because she was so scared, but God started reminding her of His promise of protection for her family. So for two hours she walked the floor and told the devil that she was not going to receive that report because it did not agree with God's Promise, and she started praising God for her son's safety.

Then she called the senator's office, and said, *"I think you have made a mistake. I know my son is alive."* They told her that they would make some phone calls and then call her back. The whole time she was waiting for the call, the devil tried to tell her that her son was dead, but she was determined not to listen to that voice in her head.

Finally, the phone call came, and they started apologizing for making such a terrible mistake. They had found out that her son was indeed alive and well. When you trust God and refuse to let fear thoughts change your mind, you will see God do miracles for you and your family.

***

The more you trust God, believe His Word and choose to love Him and walk close to Him—the more you will get rid of the fear that something bad is going to happen to your loved ones. One of my biggest fears used to be that one of my family members would get sick and die or be killed in an accident. When I found this promise in Psalm 91, I started thanking God every morning for the protection over my family. I thanked Him that I didn't have to be afraid any longer, because I knew He would not make a promise if it were not true.

Finally the time came that the fears went away, and peace came in my heart.

Some time later Jack and I drove to the country with our son to feed sixty large, hungry Brahma cows. Bill took the sack of feed and started running in front of the cows as the feed poured out on the ground, but they didn't see the feed on the ground. They just saw Bill running with the feed sack on his shoulder, so they started chasing him until it looked like they all ran right over the top of him. The devil told me that he had been trampled to death like a cowboy in a stampede.

Fears came all over me, but then the Lord reminded me of this promise in verse ten. I started thanking God out loud that *I would not be afraid, because no tragedy would come near my family.* And God did a miracle. Even though those cows were running so fast that they couldn't stop, some way God parted the cows. They ran around him instead of over the top of him, and he was safe.

Chapter 12

Angels, Angels, Angels
♫ ♫ ♫

He will put His angels in charge of you. They will watch over you wherever you go. They will catch you with their hands. And you will not hit your foot on a rock. Psalm 91: 11-12

The Bible talks about God's angels all through the Old and the New Testament. They are mighty beings—so strong that one angel can overcome more than a thousand men. They are ready at all times to carry out God's will and to watch over God's people.

Angels are spirits who serve God and are sent to help those who will receive salvation.
Hebrews 1: 14

Have you ever been fishing on a lake in the middle of the night? Some people think that is the very best time to catch fish. When my husband was seven years old, all the people who worked for his father took their boats to Lake Brownwood to do some night fishing. Jack was placed in a boat with five adults so he would be well supervised. Since one of the men in the boat was an expert swimmer, his mother and dad thought he would especially be in good hands.

Later that night during one of the times when the boats were going back and forth to shore for bait, Jack had gotten out of his boat and into another one without anyone seeing him. Then off they went—without Jack—back onto the lake in the dark. This was back before there were rules about life jackets and lights on your fishing boats, so no one could see in the dark what actually happened. Perhaps they hit a stump, but for some reason the boat Jack had been in sank. All five of the people in it drowned, even the expert swimmer. It became obvious that Jack had been directed to another boat by *angels who serve God and are sent to help those who will receive salvation.*

***

In 1968, while my brother-in-law, Lloyd, was in the service, he and my sister, Sandra, and their new baby, Rhonda, were stationed in Fürth, Germany. For those of you who like to ride bicycles—you would have loved it there. Practically everyone rode bicycles everywhere they went, but the bikes in Germany—especially back in the 60's—were not made for safety. Babies were carried in a basket type seat on the front of the bicycle with no cushions and no safety straps to hold them in. When Rhonda was nine months old, she was in

Sandra's bike carrier as they crossed a very narrow, railroad bridge with a pedestrian lane over the Regnitz River. It was pretty nerve racking to drive her bike on that narrow walkway with the low side rails that gave very little protection from the 50 ft drop to the water below, but she never dreamed of the real danger they were facing. About half way across she ran her front tire into the rail—throwing Rhonda head first out of the basket & over the railing. Sandra said that panic surged through her entire body as she watched her baby flying through the air. But suddenly, it was as though an unseen force thrust her hand out over the rail—just in time to grab the little snowsuit that Rhonda was wearing. Another split second and she would have plunged to the water below, and there would have been no way to get off the bridge and down to the water in time to save her, even if she had survived the fall. God's angels were definitely on duty that day. Sandra and Lloyd have never doubted those angels being right there—watching over their little one. If not, Rhonda would never have survived to be serving the Lord like she is today.

See that you do not despise one of these little ones, for I say to you, that their angels in heaven contin-ually behold the face of My Father who is in heaven.
Matthew 18: 10

We have a friend named Mr. Bowers who was working in the mines in Clovis, New Mexico, setting off the explosives. One particular day he was ready to set off the charge, when someone tapped him on the shoulder. To his surprise, no one was anywhere around. Deciding that it must have been his imagination, he started once again to push the plunger when he felt another tap on his shoulder. Again, no one was there, so he decided to move all the equipment several hundred feet back up the tunnel. When he finally set off the explosion, the whole top of the tunnel caved in exactly where he had been standing. Do you think he just happened, by accident, to move out of the pathway of destruction? You could never make our friend believe that. He knew it was an angel who tapped him on the shoulder that day.

Angels are just as real as you and me, and when you speak God's Word, the angels obey. That is because they were created to obey the voice of God's Word. You are leaving the angels out of your life when you say negative things that do not agree with the Bible.

Bless the Lord, you His angels, Mighty in strength, who perform His word, obeying the voice of His Word!   Psalm 103: 20

Chapter 13

The Enemy Can't Hurt Me!
📖 📖 📖

You will walk on the lion and cobra... and the serpent (dragon KJV) you will trample down.(NAS)
Psalm 91: 13

Does this verse mean that you will really walk on top of a lion and on top of a snake? No! God is painting a picture so you can understand the authority you have. Do you know what authority means? Let me give you an example: No one is surprised when a policeman stops a person who is driving too fast and gives him a ticket. That's because a policeman is given the *right* to do that. When someone has authority—that means they have the *"right"* to do certain things.

The *lion*, the *cobra* and the *dragon* are word pictures to describe Satan and his demon spirits. The *lion* is a picture of when Satan comes after you loud and bold. One example might be when someone tries to pick a fight with you and hits you and hurts you for no reason. That is an attack that is coming at you boldly—face on—like a lion.

The *cobra* snake is a picture of when Satan sneaks up on you and tries to hurt you when you least expect it. For example, when someone tells lies about you behind your back. It is not the person who is your enemy. It is Satan who is using that person's mouth.

You might have guessed what the lion and the cobra stood for, but what are *dragon* problems? In the *Strong's Bible Concordance* the word also means *sea monster.* You know that there is no such thing as a dragon or a sea monster. Dragons are made up in a person's imagination—so why is that listed, when it's not real? God put that illustration there on purpose. *Dragon* fears represent *fears that are not real.* Have you ever been afraid of something that was not real? I knew one young teenager who would wake up in the middle of the night and get fearful when she saw one of her sister's dolls.

If someone is fearing something that is not real—that sounds harmless enough. But if a person believes it, that kind of fear can do as much damage as the fear of something that *is* real. For example: maybe there was a time when you were afraid of the dark! That's a *dragon* fear because the dark can't hurt anyone. But even if it's not real, the fear itself will still do damage to your body and your mind. It is the fear that will hurt you, much more than the thing you're afraid of. That is why

God tells you *not to be afraid*. Imaginary fears can make you act very strangely. One child who was afraid of the dark would crawl into the corner of the room and cover herself with an umbrella.

Some people are afraid of the sound of thunder... Some are afraid of water... That's why it's *Good News* when God tells you that you can tread on *all* the powers of the enemy. That means that they cannot hurt you, if you know your rights. You have been given the right (the authority) in Jesus' Name to overcome Satan—whether he comes after you like a *bold lion fear*, like a *sneaky snake fear* or like an *imaginary dragon fear*. Whichever way he comes, he won't hurt you when you use your authority (your God given right) in Jesus' Name and tell those fears to go.

> *Those who believe will be able to do these things as proof: They will use My Name to force demons out of people... They will touch the sick, and the sick will be healed.* Mark 16:17, 18b

My grandson, Avery Adams, is four years old and lives in Montana. His mother and daddy have taught him to take authority over sickness by saying—*by the stripes of Jesus I am healed.* Now, instead of running to his mommy every time he gets hurt, you can hear him say, *"Devil, you can't hurt me—by Jesus' stripes I am heale*d." Or sometimes you can hear him say, *"pain leave in Jesus' Name"*—and then he will usually go right on playing. It is sometimes hard to believe that someone that young knows to do that, but it is because his parents are teaching him at an early age that he has authority and rights over sickness and accidents.

Chapter 14

Do I Love God?
♥♥♥

*The Lord says, "If someone loves me, I will deliver
him.*   Psalm 91: 14

In verses 14 through 16 God Himself starts
talking to you directly. And He offers seven more
promises to anyone who truly loves Him. Ask
yourself, *"Do I really love the Lord?"* Be honest!
God already knows the answer anyway.

Do you remember when Jesus asked Peter in
John 21: 15, *"Peter, do you love Me?"* Think how
embarrassed Peter must have felt when Jesus asked
him over and over, *"Peter do you love Me?"* God
is asking you that question because He has some
wonderful promises for the one who truly loves
Him. And remember that the Lord said in John 14:
15, *"If you love Me, you will obey Me."* Your
obedience shows you if you really do love God.

The whole reason we were created is so that we
could be best friends with the Lord. When David
was just a shepherd boy, he would be out in the
field at night watching over his sheep—playing his
harp and singing love songs to the Lord. And do

you remember what God said about David. God called him, "*a man after My own heart.*" There is nothing that God wants from you as much as He wants you to spend time talking to Him, listening to Him and having fellowship with Him. The more time you spend with God, the more you will learn to trust Him and know that His Word is true. David learned to trust God, and that is why he was not afraid to fight the lion and the bear—and later, the giant. God had become his best friend, and he knew that *God would never leave nor forsake him.*

It is so important to daily spend time alone with God. When our grandchildren, Cullen and Meritt, stay the night with us, the moment they finish breakfast they each run to his own secret place to spend some time talking with God. Start making that a habit every morning. Find a place that is just yours and the Lord's. That special, alone time with God will cause you to love Him more and better understand His great love for you. So ask yourself if you love God, because if you do, then **THESE PROMISES ARE FOR YOU.**

The first promise is for deliverance. God will deliver you from all the things that we have been talking about—accidents, disease, natural disasters and bad things that people would try to do to harm you! Thank God for His promise to deliver you.

Nothing is impossible with God! (NAS) Luke 1: 37

Jesus says, "Meet Me at our secret place!"

Chapter 15

I Am Seated With Christ Jesus

Because he has loved me…I will set him securely
on high, because he has known My Name.
Psalm 91: 14b

To be able to *sit with God in heavenly places* is the second promise to those who *love God* and *know Him by name.*

He has raised us up with Him (Jesus), and seated
us with Him in heavenly places, in Christ Jesus.
(NAS) Ephesians 2: 6

What does it mean to be seated with Christ in heavenly places? When God raised Jesus from the dead, He made Him more important than anything in this world or in the next world. There is nothing or no one who is more important than Jesus. God put everything under His power. He also made Him head over the Church which is His Body. Then Jesus gave His authority over every thing in this world to us Christians to use in His Name. So if He is seated above everything on earth—when we walk in His ways and do His will, we are above everything too. All the evil in this world is under our feet.

Think what it is like to be seated with Christ in heavenly places. When we realize where we are sitting spiritually, it gives us a whole new outlook. When you were little, did you ever go to a parade and not be able to see any of the floats because of all the people in front of you? That happened to me once, and I remember my father picking me up and putting me on his shoulders. It was wonderful because from that high up, I was able to see the whole parade—and not just the part that was passing right in front of me. I could also look all the way down the street and see what had already passed and what was coming. That's what God does for us. When He seats us with Christ Jesus in heavenly places, we are no longer blinded spiritually. We can see things the way God sees them—from His heavenly perspective.

What does verse 14 mean when it says that we have known His Name? When God wanted to show the people something important about Himself or about His promises in the Old Testament, He would make it known by telling the people another one of His Names. For example, when He wanted Abraham to know that He would provide everything that Abraham would ever need, God told Abraham that His Name was Jehovah-Jireh, which means *I am the Lord who provides.*

God wanted the Israelites to know that He was their healer, so He told them that His Name was Jehovah-Rapha, which means *I am the Lord who heals*. There are many names of God, and each of those names tells us something else that God will do for us—Jehovah-Shalom: *the Lord our Peace,* Jehovah-Tsidkenu: *the Lord our Righteousness,* Jehovah-Raah: *the Lord our Shepherd,* Jehovah-Nissi: *the Lord our Banner (protector)*...

This is not a complete list of all of God's Names, but it is an example of how God has always painted a picture of Himself, His character and His promises through one of His Names. For example, if I told you that the neighbor who lived next door on my right was *the mechanic*, the neighbor on my left was *the dentist,* the neighbor across the street was *the grocer* and the neighbor down the street was *the doctor*, you would immediately know a lot about my neighbors without my saying anything else. That is how each name of God tells us a great deal about Him.

Chapter 16

God Answers When I Call!
███

They will call on Me, and I will answer them.
Psalm 91: 15a

The third bonus promise from God is to answer those who truly *love Him* and *call on His name.* If we ask something in Jesus' Name, it has to be according to His will, because His Name and His Will and His Word are the same.

We can come to God with no doubts. This means that when we ask God for things (and if those things agree with what God wants for us), then God cares about what we say. God listens to us every time we ask Him. So we know that He gives us the things that we ask from Him.
I John 5: 14-15

Just think about what that verse is saying to you. Do you realize that every time you pray **a prayer that lines up with God's Word,** He hears you? And because He hears you, you can know that He will give you whatever you ask. Wow! That one promise should keep us always trying to find out what God's Word says so we can pray exactly according to His Will.

I am going to let James Zintgraff, our associate pastor's son, tell this next miracle in his own words:

The Summer that Cullen was five years old, I was swimming with him and his cousins in their pool. One of the adults had said, "OK, everyone out of the pool." Everyone else had headed inside the house when Cullen saw a plastic life raft come floating by. He said, "Hey, James, watch this," as he stepped off the side of the pool onto the raft like it was a solid piece. It flipped out from under him, and he fell backwards into the water, grazing his head on the side of the pool as he fell.

It was the deep end of the pool, and I watched Cullen, with his arms and legs outstretched, just start sinking to the bottom. I dived in and grabbed him under the arms, but he is unusually big for his age—and weighed more than I did. His dad always said that he felt like a chunk of lead when you tried to lift him, so I wondered if I could get him to the top of the water—especially since he must have been dazed from scrapping his head on the concrete.

I knew we were in trouble so I called on God, and suddenly, I felt someone grab me from behind and begin pushing Cullen and me straight up from the bottom of the pool. (I thought one of the adults had seen us and dived in to help me.) I shot up out of the water with Cullen above me. Then it was like someone pulled Cullen from my arms and laid him on the side of the pool. (I was in water way over my head, so there was no way I could have lifted dead weight out of the pool.) Cullen started crying and coughing, and when I looked around, no one was there—absolutely, no one! I knew *God had heard me call,* and He had sent an angel to *answer my call.*

By this time the adults came running out of the house to see if we were OK. They treated me like a hero, and I was given a plague that says, "James Zintgraff saved Cullen Ruth's life," but I knew that I could not have done that rescue alone. I was only an eleven year old kid. I know that God heard me and sent His angel to answer my call.

James Zintgraff

The next time you are in the deep end of a swimming pool, try getting under someone and lifting him out of the water—without touching the sides or bottom of the pool. It is next to impossible. Trained lifeguards would have difficulty doing what James did, but his secret was *calling on God.* And God was big enough to lift both Cullen and James.

***

One day we came home and found that the car belonging to our teenagers had been stolen from the carport. When we prayed and asked God to return the car, He told us to choose to forgive the one who took it. That was hard at first, but we remembered that forgiveness is a choice, not a feeling, and we made a sincere choice to forgive the person who had taken from us. Forgiving them didn't seem to help the situation. The sheriff's department told us that they didn't think we would ever see that car again since it had been gone for almost a week. It was hard to ignore that negative report, but we just kept believing that God would do a miracle. We knew that even if we never saw that car again, we would still love and trust God, but we didn't want the devil to win. And sure enough, after one week a man turned himself in and said that he had stolen things all of his life, but this was *the first time he had ever felt guilty.*

He told us that he had left the car on the parking lot of the rodeo grounds. When we drove up, there it was—exactly where he had said. **We called on God, and, just like He promised, He answered.**

Chapter 17

God Rescues Me From Trouble!
☺☺☺

I will be with them in trouble and I will rescue them.
Psalm 91: 15

The fourth promise to the one who loves God is
to be *rescued from trouble.* Have you ever been in
trouble and needed to be rescued? When I think of
God rescuing us when we are in trouble, I always
think of this story.

We had a flood in Brownwood several years
ago, and Bill had a herd of goats on the land by the
river. The flood waters came up so quickly that
the water overflowed the banks, and his goats had
no way to get to higher ground. Thankfully, some
old ranchers happened to see them and were able
to get them hoisted up into the loft of a barn before
they drowned.

It was so deep and swift by the time Bill got to
the edge of those flood waters that the police
wouldn't allow anyone through the road blocks.
Thinking the goats had been washed away in the
flood, you can imagine how happy Bill was when
someone told him that they were in the top of a

barn across the river. He knew, however, that they would suffocate—all closed up in that loft with no water and hardly any air—if he didn't get to them soon. So he found a little tin bottom boat and went out across those dangerously swift, flood waters to rescue his goats that were in trouble.

Bill had bottle fed one of the goats after its mother had died and named him *'Little Willie'*. As Bill got close to the barn, he recognized Little Willie's voice calling to him louder than all the others. It took a while to get the loft door open while standing in the boat with the water rushing by on each side—but the moment it came loose, Little Willie was the first one to jump into his arms. Bill was able to pull the goats down into the boat a few at a time, and then—boat load by boat load—he rowed them all back to safety.

There was a TV crew from Abilene filming the flood, and Bill and his goats made a great news story that day. Everyone on the six o'clock news, and then again at ten o'clock, watched the little goat boy as he rescued all of his goats.

I never think of Bill rescuing those goats that were in trouble, without thinking of how God sees us, like Little Willie, calling out in our troubles. And when we do, God always finds a way to rescue us. Aren't you thankful that we have a loving heavenly Father who rescues us out of our troubles? Whatever trouble you find yourself in, remember that nothing is too big for God. But you have to run to Him—not away from Him.

***

Another time Bill tried to swim across a lake that was much wider than he had thought. Bill, with no strength left in his body, had already gone under the water twice and was sure that he would drown. There was no one anywhere close, and even if there had been, he could never have swum out that far and pulled Bill to shore. But God did a miracle. A lady came outside on the opposite bank and threw a life ring. There was no way to throw it that far, but some way—when Bill's head came out of the water for probably the last time—the life ring had made it over thirty yards. There it was—within inches of his almost lifeless body. That was certainly Bill's day of *trouble,* and we are so thankful that God was with him and *rescued* him from destruction.

Sometimes a person will think something like that is just a lucky break. When we are trusting God, there are no lucky breaks. It is God seeing us in *trouble* and coming to our *rescue.*

Chapter 18

God Honors Me!
🏆🏆🏆

I will honor them.   Psalm 91: 15

The fifth promise to those who love God is to be honored. Do you like to be honored? Of course you do! Maybe you can remember a time when a teacher called your name in school and bragged on the homework you turned in. That made you feel good. That was an honor.

Most schools have an Awards Day and different students are given special awards. When your name is called out, and an award is handed to you in front of all the other students, it is an honor. Cullen was thrilled when his teacher called him up last year and gave him a special award.

A number of years ago our daughter, Angelia, and her husband, David, attended a political rally in our city given for George W. Bush when he was campaigning for Texas Governor. She had talked to Mr. Bush at the beginning of the meeting, but after that, he had met several hundred other people before making his speech. Later, when he was leaving, everyone was shocked when he left the group he was with to come back to our daughter and thank her for something she had said. It honored her that he not only remembered her, but also remembered their conversation. He promised that he would not make her cry at the election in November.

We all like to be honored. But have you ever thought about what it means to be honored by God? How does God honor you? He honors you when He calls you His son or His daughter. He honors you every time He answers your prayer. He honors you by promising to let you live with Him eternally. There are no honors on this earth that can compare to being honored by God. I challenge you to live a life that is honored by God.

Chapter 19

God Satisfies Me with a Long Life

With a long life I will satisfy him...(NAS) Psalm 91: 16a

The sixth promise is that God will give the one who loves Him a long, full life. God does not want us to just have a lot of birthdays. Some people have had a great many birthdays, but they were never happy. God says that He will give you many birthdays, and, as those birthdays roll around, you will be satisfied and feel complete.

Everyone has an empty place inside of his heart, and nothing will fill that emptiness except Jesus. People down through the ages have tried to fill it with different things, but the things of this world will not bring lasting satisfaction. Only after you decide to follow fully after God and give Him your whole heart, will He fill your life to over flowing. Then you will experience a joy that you don't even have words to describe.

He (God) satisfies me with good things...Psalm 103:5

Bill, of course, is grown now, but when he was in his teens God spoke to him that he was going to be given a palomino horse that enjoyed being ridden, and someone would come to know the Lord because of the horse. At first we wondered if Bill might be trying to trick us by telling us that someone would come to know the Lord, but it turned out to be quite true. A Christian man who bred racehorses (we had never known of the man before) heard about Bill and decided to give him a horse as a *seed faith offering.* (A seed faith offering is something you give, and, like any seed, it multiplies back.) Everyone was shocked when the horse came, except Bill—he knew God had promised.

It was a beautiful palomino, and Bill told everyone at church about his miracle. We didn't know there was a fifteen year old girl in church that day, who, like her father, didn't believe in God. After she heard Bill's testimony, however, she told her mother that she could believe in a God like that, and she accepted Jesus as her savior.

Two of the three things that God had told Bill had come to pass—the mare was a beautiful palomino, and someone had accepted Jesus because of the horse. The only problem was that the mare did not like to be ridden. She would buck or take off running—anything to get the rider off her back. We were discouraged. We wondered why God had only brought two of the promises to pass. I kept thinking, "*Lord, it would not have been any harder for You to have given him a horse that liked to be ridden—especially since that was one of the things You told him.*" (When something happens that you don't understand, don't get angry with God or quit faithfully serving Him. Stay faithful, and God will give you the answer.)

One day Bill said that God had told him to have the mare bred; and from the moment the new colt was born, it was obvious that this was the horse that God had been planning for Bill. *Jim Dandy* loved Bill from the first moment on, and when it came time to break him for riding, he never even attempted to buck—not even once.

Years later when Bill would come home from college, he could throw a saddle on Jim Dandy, after months of not being ridden, and ride him all over the pastures. It was like they had never missed a day. If we love God and continue to serve Him, He does indeed satisfy our lives with good things.

But too often we try to satisfy ourselves instead of letting God satisfy us. Did you know that the more we love the Lord, the more unselfish we become? For example, on your birthday—what do you think about? Most of the time we're thinking about what we can do to please ourselves, and how many gifts we'll be getting. Maybe you've already made out a long list of things you want. But have you ever had a birthday when *you* gave a gift *to everyone else*?

Last year a lady from Minnesota called me to say that she was going to have a birthday party to celebrate her hundredth birthday. She wanted to buy several hundred Psalm 91 books to give to each of her friends who came to her party. Most people would be thinking about the big party and all the gifts they would be getting—especially on their 100th birthday—but this lady was thinking about everyone else. That is a good example of someone who has lived a long, satisfied life—and you can't get that kind of satisfaction any other way, except by walking closely to Jesus.

Chapter 20

I Can See God's Salvation
†††

They will see how I can save. Psalm 91: 16b

Many people are surprised when they look up the word *saved* or *salvation* in the Bible. Do you know what it means? Most people just think it means a *ticket to get into heaven.* It means that, but it means so much more. The word salvation also means *health, healing, deliverance, protection, and provision.* That means you can live in *health,* but if you happen to get sick, then God will give you *healing.* It means that He will *deliver* you from evil things that are causing you to be unhappy. He will *protect* you from harm, and He will *provide* everything you need to have a full life. A person who doesn't know God might think this is impossible, but that is just because he doesn't know the faithfulness of our powerful God.

As you learn how to trust God for His healing and deliverance and protection, other people will watch you and start learning how to trust God too. We had been teaching the people at church how to believe God's promises in Psalm 91 for protection and some of those men were helping Jack to build a coffee house for the college students. One day while they were all working there was an explosion that sounded like a bomb blew up. Fire started flying out the top of the electric power pole and steam came pouring out of the ground where they had dug a hole to pour cement.

One of the men was standing in water from the last night's rain and holding a metal stake in place while another man accidentally drove it into the main electric power line carrying seven thousand, two hundred volts of electricity. Can you even imagine how much electrical power that is? It knocked all the electricity off for blocks around, *yet neither man was hurt.* Jack had prayed just that morning for the protection of all the workers.

Many people have been killed from just playing around with a small electrical outlet in a room. The voltage running through that line was many, many times more powerful than that, yet God's salvation (His health, provision and protection) had saved their lives that day. The years of quoting Psalm 91 over our church body had certainly paid off.

***

There are promises all through the Bible, but this is the only place where all of the promises of protection are gathered together in one chapter.

Psalm 91 is a *covenant* (promise) of protection for any of God's children who will love Him and trust Him to do what He says. The world gives us a 911 number to call if we get in trouble, but God has done better than that. He has given us Psalm 91:1.

My prayer is that you will use this book as a handbook and study this Psalm 91 until every fear is driven out of your life. God wants you to know that He will be faithful to bring about every one of these promises, if you will be faithful to Him.

Picture Album

Mother & Dad, story page 11
Peggy Joyce, Jim, Sandra

Mother & Dad, story page 11
Peggy Joyce, Jim, Sandra

Sandra, Jim & Peggy Joyce
Jim's story page 24

Jack & his dog "Tippy"

T
H
R
E
E

G
E
N
E
R
A
I
O
N
S

Bill & his dog "Zooie"

Cullen & his dog "Samson"

Angie riding grandad's goats
story a generation later page 92

Great Granddad Smith
Bill & Angie

Bill & friend frog

Bill & Angie selling
Pepsi story page 41

Bill & Jim Dandy
story page 102

Bill helping work
the cows, story page 64

Jack, Peggy Joyce and Married Children

Jack & Peggy Joyce

Angelia & David

Bill & Sloan

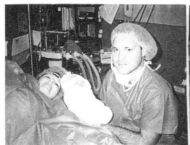

Cullen's miracle birth
story page 20

Cullen & Meritt

Cullen & Meritt
story page 80

Meritt

Cullen & Meritt
with pet turtle

Cullen the fisherman

Bill & pet tiger
fire story page 55

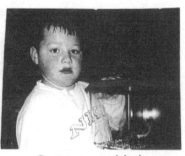

Cullen & pet bird

Cullen & friend frog

Cullen honored with
Award, story page 97

James Zintgraff &
Cullen, story page 88

Rhonda Ford
story page 68

Jolena, Heath & Avery
Adams, story, page 75

Julie & father, Dr. Crow
story page 19

Peyton Adams
Avery's baby sister

Ginger & Christy
Zintgraff, story page 34

7,200 volts of electricity
story page 107

Jeffery Phillips
story page 62

Skylar (center) & brothers
story page 54

What Must I do to be Saved?

We've talked about physical protection. Now I want us to think just a moment about eternal protection. The promises from God are for God's children who love Him. If you have never given your life to Jesus and accepted Him as your Lord and Savior, please read the following scriptures very carefully.

There is no one without sin. None!   Romans 3: 10

All people have sinned and are not good enough for God's glory.   Romans 3: 23

God loves you and gave His life that you might live eternally with Him.

But Christ died for us while we were still sinners. In this way God shows His great love for us. Romans 5: 8

For God loved the world so much that He gave His only Son so that whosoever believes in Him may not be lost but have eternal life.   John 3: 16

There is nothing we can do to earn our salvation or to make ourselves good enough for heaven. It's a free gift.

When someone sins, he earns what sin pays—death. But God gives us a free gift—life forever in Christ Jesus our Lord.   Romans 6: 23

There is also no other way that a person can reach heaven, other than through Jesus—God's Son.

Jesus is the only One who can save people. His Name is

the only power in the world that has been given to save people. And we must be saved through Him. Acts 4: 12

Jesus said, "I am the Way, the Truth and the Life; no one comes to the Father, but through Me." John 14: 6

You must believe that Jesus is the Son of God, that He died on the cross for your sins, and that He rose again on the third day.

Jesus was declared with power to be the Son of God by the resurrection from the dead. Romans 1: 4

You may be thinking, "How do I accept Jesus and become His child?" God in His Love has made it so easy.

If you use your mouth to say, "Jesus is Lord," and if you believe in your heart that God raised Jesus from the dead, then you will be saved. Romans 10: 9

As many as received Jesus, to them He gave the right to become children of God, even to those who believe in His Name. John 1: 12

It is as simple as praying a prayer similar to this one—if you sincerely mean it in your heart:

Dear God:
I confess that I am a sinner and I deserve to go to hell. But I believe that Jesus died for me, that He shed His blood to pay for my sins and that You raised Him from the dead so that I can be Your child and live with You eternally in heaven. I am asking Jesus to come into my heart and save me this very moment.
I thank You, Dear Lord, for loving me and saving me. Take my life and use it for Your Glory. *In Jesus' Name*

You don't have to wait until you are grown to share these scriptures with your friends. God expects you to start spreading the *Good News* the moment you accept Jesus into your life. Let me tell you how Bill shared these scriptures with a friend. The summer after he was in the fourth grade he had taken every one of these scriptures on salvation and marked them in his Bible. Later he had a friend named Shane who came to spend the night, and the boys wanted to put up their tent and sleep in the back yard.

Right before bedtime Jack decided that he would slip outside and check on the boys. We half expected to find them sound asleep, but to our surprise there was a light on in the tent so Jack went over very quietly and peered in. There was Bill with his flashlight and his Bible, reading these scriptures to his friend and telling him how to be saved. We slipped back into the house and had barely gotten into bed when suddenly the back door flew open and both boys came flying onto our bed with Bill saying, *"Dad, wake up! We need you to pray. Shane wants to get saved."* Bill could easily have lead him in a prayer to receive Jesus, but he had done the main part—showing him the scriptures and sharing the *Good News* that God has made a way for everyone to come to Him.

God wants all people to be saved. And He wants every one to know the Truth. I Timothy 2: 4

Do the latest statistics on cancer & other dread diseases send a chill of fear down your spine?

Do thoughts of terrorist attacks & chemical warfare cause your heart to skip a beat?

What about all the natural disasters that are striking in unexpected places?

Do you sometimes wonder if there is any safe place in the world to hide?

If any of these things has ever troubled your mind—**Peggy Joyce Ruth's book *Psalm 91 God's Umbrella of Protection for adults*** gives God's answer to every one of these questions.

Psalm 91 God's Umbrella of Protection is a comprehensive, verse by verse look at God's Covenant of Protection for adults. Ongoing tragedies, numerous terrorist threats, dread diseases, natural disasters of all kinds... are compelling people to look for a protection. The solution to these problems can be found in this book.

$8 plus $2 S&H. Call toll free: 1-877-97-books

IS THERE A YEARNING IN YOUR HEART TO TRUST GOD MORE?

Those Who Trust the Lord Shall Not Be Disappointed has the potential of building a trust in God like nothing you have ever read. Deep down, we direct our disappointments toward God—thinking that somehow He let us down. We trust God for our **eternal** life; why then can we not trust Him amid the adversities of **daily** life? Peggy Joyce Ruth has a unique way of showing that victorious living depends upon our unwavering trust in God. She demonstrates with scores of personal experiences just how faithful God really is and details how you can develop that kind of trust which will not disappoint.

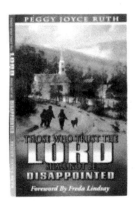

THOSE WHO TRUST IN THE LORD SHALL NOT BE DISAPPOINTED
is a comprehensive study on developing a TRUST that cannot be shaken.

$8 plus $2 S& H. Call 325 646 6894 or 1-877-97-books

PSALM 91 FOR YOUTH

To order additional copies with credit card call:
Phone: 325 646-6894
or Toll Free: (877) 97-BOOKS (877 972-6657)
or
send $8.00* each plus $2.00 shipping for 1 to 4 books**
to
The Peggy Joyce Ruth BETTER LIVING Ministries
P.O. Box 1549
Brownwood, TX, 76804-1549

*Texas residents, add 6.25% sales tax
**call 325 646-6894 for postage cost
when ordering 5 books or more

Impac Chris tian Books

332 Leffingwell Ave., Suite 101
Kirkwood, MO 63122

AVAILABLE AT YOUR LOCAL BOOKSTORE, OR YOU MAY
ORDER DIRECTLY. Toll-Free, order-line only M/C, DISC,
or VISA 1-800-451-2708.

Visit our Website at *www. impactchristianbooks.com*

Write for *FREE* Catalog.